Death and the River

Death and the River

RON HOUCHIN

SALMON POETRY

Published in 1997 by
Salmon Publishing Ltd,
Cliffs of Moher, Co. Clare

A catalogue record for this book is available from the British Library.

Salmon Publishing gratefully acknowledges the
financial assistance of the Arts Council.

ISBN 1 897648 Softcover
ISBN 1 897648 Hardcover

Cover design by Brenda Dermody of Estresso
Set by Siobhán Hutson
Printed by Redwood Books, Kennet Way, Trowbridge, Wiltshire

To Jessie, Theo, Paula, and Jim

Acknowledgements

Acknowledgements are due to the editors of the following
publications in which many of these poems first appeared:

Acorn (Ireland); *Appalachian Heritage*; *Cincinnati Poetry Review*;
Clockwatch Review; *The Courage of Animals*; *Cumberland Poetry
Review*; *Down the River*; *The Gamut*; *Grab-A-Nickel*; *Green's
Magazine*; *The Guyandotte Poets*; *The Hemingway Days Festival
Booklet*; *Kansas Quarterly*; *Lullwater Review*; *Mss*; *Painted Bride
Quarterly*; *Pearl*; *Poet Lore*; *Poetry Ireland Review*; *Puerto Del Sol*;
Quickenings; *River Poems*; *Riverstone*; *Southern Poetry Review*;
Sycamore; *The Third Wind*; *Wascana Review*; *Willow Springs*.

Grateful acknowledgement is also given to WMMT radio
station of Appalshop, Whitesburg, KY, where 'The Sadness
of Onions' was first aired.

Contents

The Life of Summer

1.

Nursing the feeling
of being left behind
when summer moves on
around the planet,
I watch the brown hares
lop about the lot
like tired beagles.
They wait under the mango
for sun to make another move.

2.

No air moves.
Taffeta leaves
listen in trees.
The sun pours
bleach on my hair and eyes.

3.

Pawpaws explode
in the grass,
blackberries stink
of cucumber.

4.

The life of summer
escapes.
My sandal flattens
a snake's skin on the walk.

Apple Time

These are the women who never married
or never wanted to. These are women
never pared down to suit a man, the women
who hung around to overripeness.
Beauty bulges in their rosy cheeks.

This is their time in the straight wooden chairs,
wielding a knife, at an old door
turned flat for a table.
This is their time to sit like queens of Hybla
surrounded by gatherers whose bodies are burdened
with the beauty and nectar of apples.

This is the time these women go forward
in brown butters, thick pies, dark ciders,
and red chips of apple peel candies.
It is time to give in
to the obvious fecundity of the season.

The jars are ready,
the walls are stacked with tall baskets,
the town stands around outside.
Above the women's busy hands,
their smiles bloom. To them the future
is red, round and as comfortable as an orchard.

Mushroom

Whatever it was the world
used to do with these knobs
has lost its vacuum, broken,
frayed its wirings.
The eldritch engineers have disappeared.

Perhaps they are connected to us.
When we turn or trample or eat them,
they click on in our heads,
and we mythologise, divagate, or opine.

Whole ones in spaghetti encourage
creativity. Hers stood on the table
becomes a sashaying square dancer.
Mine fisted and fed to her across the table
becomes the helmet of an ancient penis.

The shape of the mushroom influences
doorknobs, umbrellas, the miniature
acreage of the manure pile, night clouds,
atomic-death belches, and things that
spring up over night.

Even the tall shadows of Chicago
tarnish the silver of evening skies.

A Stone's Song

The damn thing has stopped
Its shimmering under the sun, has
Turned to stone again, reluctant,
Quiet, retentive under the dotted swiss
Of the deepening sky.

Its music comes on solidly, like silence.
I get out of bed hearing the stone, hating it for
Its clandestine knowledge, its stolid
Learning, its way, its mocking cer-
Tainty, its harmony.

Mindlessly, I toy with chiselling it into
A picnic table. But it's too small.
I could never bear its song
Mutilated, when what music I have deforms, caco-
Phonises, ephemerates, and sloughs off in slumber
All too soon to matter.

I go out to it with a hammer
And a geology text. I turn to
The chapter on origins and beg
In silence, its native tongue,
'I know you, see.'
But it knows better.
Its tune continues, stone-deaf
Cadences sinking into the sym-
Phonic night.

Frontier

Under the sweet potato clouds,
Dust, like locust,
Swarms around the eyes of the only man
In a thousand miles. He squints,
Like a tiger, his oxygen eyes on the lines
Of civilisation in the sky.
Driftwood hands loaf on the shore
Of his pockets.
Smoke, like a grandmother's braid,
Lets down from the chimney of his soddy.
Chickens frozen like commas
In the dirt yard wait as for some word
From the wind. A coyote passes over
The carpet of the hills.
The tracks always lead toward some horizon,
Away from where civilisation circles its own ideas.
He thinks frontier and reinvents it. It never runs out.

Neither does it run up to any woman,
A woman to hold him down in bed and at the slow
Breakfast table while the horses stamp
Outside in the surprise of dawn.
Neither does it run out when it runs up to
Any ocean, an ocean to sway like a blue summer
Dress worn by his blond first cousin
Forbidden to play in the field after dark.
Neither does the frontier end with any season;
The seasons are like houses, too confining,

In December when he walks his underwear
Out for a smoke beneath the singing stars.
For him the frontier ends only when it becomes
A hollow thing sought after for inspiration only,
The wife never home for more than a smile,
A thing left about for laundry day, or
Kept up after supper for cleaning the gun,
Or lost in the bath tub like the last sliver
Of soap dug up from the bottom.
It dissolves as it's clawed for
And disappears before it reaches the surface.

The Courage of Animals

They labour their bodies like tractors;
 They never consider themselves tissue,
  Muscle or think of longevity;
   It's only blood on throats –
Where would life be without the red
 Alert – but guiltless, their hardy engines
  Run on twin cylinders
   Of hunger and fear . . . .
Where I only suspect sometimes that
 I am alive by the telltale
  Of some feeble guilt;
   They lay down the burden
Where life ends among familial
 Bones or have it cut from
  Them by hot lead and quick steel;
   Their only guilt –
You can see it in their dying eyes –
 Is the inexorable leaving
  Of life always before
   Their courage is used up.

The Drinking

Gradually, I am forgetting the walls,
gradually, beneath my clothes,
I feel a beast without certainties –
the wild, open, shifting animal
whose thoughts must prowl these woods.
I am so inarticulate now
I cannot wish or name – air or state.
What happens to it all when walls come down?
Where do I use this raw nerve ending in instinct?

The room falls apart, the sun foams in the sky,
the wind comes in to sit and stare,
the night savagely chews the mud.
I could be coming to my 'mind' again –
I could be discussing sports and politics,
safe in the culture of my own pajamas.
But I have to wake the ageing Grendel
who unsettles the cold dust in my veins.
I want to feel the ancient energy that flows
from heart to brain . . . .

And I want the times
when the lie was like a prayer,
when 'God was a fire in the head.'

The Famous Waitress

Never rests
on the way to your table.
She glides across the carpet jiggling
two glasses of water.
Her life is ennobled by its ordinariness.
She goes about it like a new nun.

She is no nun, but she is special.
We can tell. She is capable,
can fill everyone's need like a water glass.
Everyone watches her from the corner
of a menu.

She is not quite the hard prostitute,
bountiful from lust.
She is not nearly the dutiful nurse,
clear as gauze, or officious.
The famous waitress is somewhere
in between. We enjoy her promptness
and her perfume and the intimacy of tipping.

Hovering above the sirloin, she takes the trouble
to remind us of Mother asking about our food.
        Who would break this woman's heart
and ruin her day. Who would say the napkin
had a disgusting spot on it,
the salt shaker was full of rice,
or the table cloth was off-centre.
But if we did, would she pull out her pocketfuls of tips
and buy off our petty complaints
with the pretty nickels of her life?

We are not related to the cashier,
where we are bound to wind up;
are not related to the manager
who stands around like Zeus;
are not related to the busboy
who grabs our coat like Vergil;
are not related to the queer loneliness
in the parking lot.

        We come back for the relationship,
for Beatrice, or Betty, who has
held up her hand and let
our wishes write on her life.

The Age of Darkness

Can we find a great column of darkness,
say, from a well capped by Adam,
and count the rings
where light leaked in?

Can we count the stars
like the hexagons on the back of a turtle?
Can we count them back to the first one
in the centre of the night's slow shell
and point and say it began there, then?

I swear the age of darkness is known
each time the sun goes down
and we stand atop the golden hills
with our silver spoons, our nervous fires,
our battery-powered portraits of the moon.

A Short History of Fire

Every night I'm in my sleeping-cave
listening to the wind
and wondering at the wolf's song
and leaning or longing toward you.

Every night you are in a crowd
knowing as little of sleep as you do of me,
wondering where your next meal's coming from,
thinking the only sleep is death,
the only death, famine – the hiss and the hum.

I had loved you long before
you met Joan D'Arc.
I loved you when I brought you home
that first cold night. Your bright eyes
took in everything and wanted it all at once.

The Long Knife

No poem fits my head
like a long knife fits my hand.
But this thing that cuts
anything it's thinner than
hates the poem left in me,
would cut it out too, if it could.
I can't write with it in my hand,
but it seems to think we're for each other.
I could go down to the edge
of the earth in moonlight,
like a devout pagan,
and carve votive circles in the sand.
I could hold this aroused steel
while the water falls all over itself,
while the night continues to amuse the darkness,
the knife continues to be about dying,
poetry continues to be about the knife,
and only death continues to be about itself.

Animal Confessions

He watches me wordlessly from positions
he's taken up for the purpose of pouring
out his hopeless situation. Black eyes
with diamonds in them at my feet, forgiveness
not on his mind, he soaks me up silently.
He's trapped. I know that; he knows, of course,
but I can't tell him ... He can only allow me
to guess as he pads over the oval rug,
circles it as if trying to come to the point.
Then, the flames reflecting from his back,
he watches me from the cell of another life,
to see if I have suspected right.
I don't bother to give him a knowing smile;
I'm not that sure he's there.
He watches me watch the late show. That flat,
constant stare is more than I can bear.
I glance at him during the commercials.
We're always waiting for one of us to think
of a way. When I say something, anything,
he says yes with his tail. I go back
to the show. Carrying sins I can't imagine,
he comes this way, head low,
wanting to try one more time –
both our tongues work to bridge the gap.

Flowers of Fire

explode out of the night soil.
They grow from across the river
till the new, July-ed sky brightens
below the hills in meek imitation of day.

The flowers shed hot seeds
that cool in the wind and fade,
giving air back to air.
They will sleep there
and grow there another year.

But now blossoms lighten
the dark self of the river:
cool bronze, metal blue, faded red.
Like a fresh child, passionate
for picking colour and shape,
my daughter stands with me in the dark,
her face just now yellow with pollen.

Night Walk

A small boy feeds fingers of a tree
to his pet fire.
Work clothes on a line
wave at something darker than the clouds.
A white bicycle with training wheels
leans exhausted at a stump.
When I walk, hands in my pockets,
head down, scraping the ceiling of dream,
everything I see is me.

Abstractions

The difficulty of
the squat woman
who wipes down the machines
in the laundromat
in becoming cleanliness –
The frustration of
the writer, in a dark study by a river
wading into the currents of night,
becoming truth –
The ease of
the boy in the blue ball cap that reads
'Ashes to ashes, dust to dust ... '
and a black t-shirt in
turning into death –
The futility
of the Dalmatian breathing into the rug
beside the warm chair, nose
reflected in the andirons, in
becoming awareness –
The patience of
the cosmos drawing space, curving
light, pinching out life, in
becoming less –

But the River

I sink into the bath,
like a river, but the river
I love steams a thousand miles
east in the morning sun.
My feet are where the river ends.
It begins where my head rests
on the cold enamel, but I have not
touched its water's birth and death.
I put a hand on each bank
in my captured river,
yet it's wider that my reach.
I stand in the river,
my toes shining among cold stones,
but never touch the bottom.
I pull the plug in my round river,
and it swallows itself with bits of me.
Now my head is in the river.
The river is in my head,
but I don't know the river.
It steams a thousand miles east
in the morning sun.

After Great Rain

The downpour stops
contemplative mists
rise from the figs
I stare out the beaded glass
as halted as the trees
What is it now
What is come   Gone
Formal things recede
A hundred silver faces
fill each pane
round orchards grow
like crystal fruit
on the limbs of light
The world ripened
to extinction
drops off

Death Notice

I wanted to write you a letter,
but you were dead.
I had no idea. I got up
some time after two
and went into the living room
that always fills with the dead.
Trying to think what to say
after all this time,
I started to read yesterday's paper.
There you were, the second obituary,
like a concentrated life.

I went out to the patio;
the house felt like a coffin.
The Earth was filled with the dead.
They rose up in the dark like heat waves
and pricked little white holes in the sky.
Two bats escaped from the moon.
I had to get away from the heat;
I went back to bed. No envelope or loss,
no postage or dream can carry the past.

Getting Out of Prison

Birds have nothing on me but wings;
soon that could change,
like the shape of the windshield.
With any luck at all,
the brick wall will strain the soul
right out of this new suit;
and at last I may know
the questions I always wanted to ask:
Is it the soul that moves the body?
What is it the world wants to be?

Gathering

This, the fat, nervous bats fluttering,
as thick as hair in the crack of the cliff;

the gentle elms fingering the sky at the road's end,
separating the lips of the air,
and the clustered leaves at the base
hugging their way into the earth;

this gathering of the elders on the porches of the Ohio
and the Mississippi and the Missouri telling
of their hard youths, before they fade like river lights,
women folding the lost edges of their crocheting up,
men flipping meteors into the corners of the yards;

the new furniture stacking up on the sidewalk,
the hired movers conferring at the back of the truck,
wiping their heads with red handkerchiefs;

the dogs' chorus accompanying the whoop and wheeze
of the siren that panics the streets and the babies –
this talking daughter in the heart of the park
and her whitened father's fingers forking his next-to-last cigar;
all this contrasting to the ticking light of the stars,
as if this having of time and this congregating of ours
could be seen through the dust of the galaxies,
as if this is all that living things can do.

Displacement
Christmas Day, 1985, Manchester, Indiana

The starlings have been breathing wood smoke all morning.
To stay warm they huddle on one of the square chimneys
    across the street.
From their height they could see the Lutheran church,
and the faithful crunching to their cars,
the pizza shop and the laundromat,
and the café-restaurant all closed up and frozen over
    like death.
When a new bird comes to the comfort of this smoky station,
there is a jostling along the top until one bird falls
and flies over to a skeletal limb
where an over-coated group leans into the wind.
Soon, impatience and freezing will bring one back,
and a different black thing will flap over to the barkless
    limb and fidget.
I sit in a grandfather chair, reading a grandfather's Bible,
the leather of its cover as soft and easy to hold
as a dying hand.
When I think of the grace and peace
leaving the back bedroom,
my comfortable ideas squint in the heat and smoke
that rise from sure death. They jostle for footing.
One that's been warm for a long time spreads
like black feathers and drifts to a cold limb and grips.

Hourglass

My friends come down
from the North and ask about the tide:
'Is it in or out?' They ask as if
they had landed in the middle
of an undiscernible season.
I always want to say something
like 'The ocean is the death
your dark rivers murmur about
in their sleep.'
But I never do.
I just bend down
to the shells that tumble up
here around our feet –
little convoluted deaths.
I pick up several to put to our ears.
I know they won't echo my name
or my friends', but the hum and hiss
that's in everything.
Then I want to pick up a handful
of sand, gritty with time, and say
'Take this with you, now.'

Small Baptism

The ugly, the bald, the fat, and the aged
are down in the river in their white shirts and suits,
like foundered clouds. They sink into the silver ripples,
still ugly when they emerge,
but shouting and screaming for change.
They are beginning to become some other,
something that God can love,
thick or thin, old or hairless.
Their bodies break open in the water
and wash down past the houses
where the untransformed are alone
with their ugliness and their age, alone with unchange.
The river is full of baptists who know
they are too big to get into heaven on feathers,
so they are down in the wide vee near the bank
waving their arms like fins and gulping down
big chunks of water and, at least for the moment,
spawning in hope. They know to climb a mountain
they must be smaller than it. Suddenly,
in the wider water, the deeper air, the heavier sky,
they are small, so goddamned small.

World of the Dead

My walls are full of their faces;
some few are in frames.
Under my foot in the earth or on the porch
or floor, they crawl like lizards.
I rest my eyes from the day's work,
and they come to the wire-glass window
like prisoners trying to get my attention.
On my high wardrobe pictures of family
gather suspicion and dust.
I rarely look into their lost eyes.
I know they are there behind the paper.
Their eyes scream that our world is rented
by the living, owned by the dead.
Each night in their blind sacks,
they whisper around my bed.
I keep my head under the covers.
I can't let them know that I know they're dead.
If I go to the kitchen for water,
they stand around me longing to swallow.
I have to make a fuss of getting up
lest they touch me or bump into my arm.
They are forbidden, too, I think,
for fear our worlds would fold into each other.
But, by day, I want to push my face
into that of my dead mother
and shout, I know you are there!
We all do, but we are careful too.
None of us knows exactly when
our world ends and yours begins.

The Deadly Mantis

is just ending on TV
again. For the past hour and a half,
she's been eating her way to me.
Still, I am nine.
From the kitchen mother yells it's time
for me to give up Science Fiction
and go to bed.
Instead, I go outside
to punish insect children
for the hours of sleep I'll lose.
The black sky is full of eyes.
Wings flutter and whine around the porch glow.
I grab a moth,
its wings almost cloth.
The powder comes off on my fingertips.
The fine stuff keeps wings soft,
connects it to the air,
and every other living moment. So
my mother yells again from a grave,
but I won't let the moth go.

The Thing Is, I Am Bread

People who are doors spread back
To let everything in untouched.
Something touches only on the way out.
Movers seem to be the ones who tear up doors.

For those who are chairs,
One great gesture is enough: a war,
An epidemic, The Depression. As still as wood,
They give up whatever is taken from them.

The people of curtain continue to keep out
Whatever would get in, spending their lives in corrugation
Before the window like a conscience.
The dull side faces out, the bright side looks in.

The brotherhood of bread is composed of soft souls
Who conspire like acrobats to be pyramids.
Mountains encourage them. They want to grow stronger
    than a box.
It is the air that reduces their billowy hopes to crumbs.

Most bricks are benefactors, simple folk
Who believe in what they can do. They fit in wherever
They go. Shunning the rustic life of rock,
They live in cities, like their ancestors.

People like cups are travellers. It takes
Strong heat and starving cold to fill their attention.
When they have a home, they seem to sit about
Useless and empty, looking for the dining car.

The Red Jeep

nothing much matters
about

a red jeep up-ended in
the median

snow flakes melting on
the hood

Ladder Trick

I stand it up against the air
in the middle of the field.
I run up a rung, then two.
The ladder starts to fall;
it doesn't know what I'm doing.
I straighten it. I flit up four
or five rungs before it begins to fall.
I'm learning the trick that began in my skin
and is thinking its way into wood.

The ladder believes it needs a wall
or a tree before a man can climb it.
It never reckoned such a boy.
The wind comes up. It helps to have
something to push and pull against.
I jump off when the ladder falls toward me.
It still doesn't know I'm going to the top.

I come back after lunch. It is lying
in the warm grass as confused as a horse.
Again I stand it up. I sense it waiting to see
what I'll do. The grey uprights feel like forearms.
The sun opens its eyes. I trip up three rungs;
it still seems willing to stand.
After the fourth, it begins to fall.
I ride it to the ground.

I lift it up and pound its legs
on the hard field. I run up one, two,
three. Back down I come. It stays quiet.
I put its arms up again. It stands
for a moment in quiet balance.

I zip to the top and throw my leg over.
Some thin clouds are coming back. I see
my house, distant for an instant like
a book left in a field. I come back to earth
only to see if we can do it again.

The White Sea

Navigation suggests somewhere to go
and some place to avoid,
but all journeys on this flat world
start due north and drift to the deep south,
start in the cold tensions of the stars
and wind up at a warm abyss.
I always see myself, a tiny black dot
reckless on the waves, ink and telescope
tumbling toward the sky.
At the end I dock, throw down my lever,
disrobe another identity,
and sleep in the whiteness.
To sleep till morning is such travel.
Dreams are made.
But I am never off this ocean; my voyage,
you are always the same: boustrephedonic,
mapless, detailed for destinations I never find.
I wake up in fear of arrival.

Waste Not, Want Not

3 a.m., she's rocking in her favourite chair,
wrapped in a ragged robe, 2 fat new ones
folded in her cedar chest, her 7 kids
safe, asleep in her memory with the one man
she ever knew, who cheated on her 6 times.
He's dead now and counting flame.

                                    3 hours
left, hours left, till the alarm sends
her out to count the cows and toss
2 buckets of corn in with their feed.
This time of morning she feels best
about what she owns. There's coal in the cellar,
enough for winter. She's in her inventory,
hiding from The Depression, when I sneak
behind her to the toilet.

                                    In her Indian eyes,
court was always in session. I think she
worshipped all numbers, but zero was the Devil.
And next to this were hunger,
pain, and plenty of nothing.
I hope
whatever's after life has no room for numbers.
I never saw her happy, hugging, or hilarious.
I doubt she could count as high as that.

Horses and High Water

The first half of December, the earthy waters
stalked up the McMurty fields.
The old man's four horses went to the high corner,
near his house, to stand sad-eyed
and brown as violins.
                         When the water
covered the bellies of his tractor and his truck,
he still did nothing, as if disbelief were a sufficient dam.
Above ground like dough, full of dreadmarks, and the horses'
sucking hooves, clouds locked into their docks.
The temperature dropped; the sky melted toward Christmas.

                         I gave up looking
out the window. The freezing rain still caught
in the horses' hair; ice landed in their lashes.
Each morning there was fresh hay in the highest
part of the lot. It is in such contrasts I hear
the carolling of despair.
                         Now, those four horses
have run far from the stable of memory.
The minute hands of snow curried everything
at midnight, saying, Remember,
there is no such thing as lost.

What the Things Say

Your black slipper goes 'Wah'
on its side. Its spouse has left
it now, run over at the heel
and dry-rotted at the top.

Your white gown has fallen down
the side of the chair. It wallows
to its own puddle on the floor.
It sleeps with other beings there.

The crooked mattress hangs like a lip
pulled grotesquely to the side.
The co-dependent mirror shows you
how all your things hover or collide.

How all your things are homeless!
Where they land is their bed.
How they are flung, planted,
or blown is the life they endure.

To them the living are just
harder hands, sharper shoulders.
Like words without breath,
your dropped socks lie formless on the floor.

The Clairvoyance of Earth

It's not just that everything
on the busy planet was becoming
something we could worship or use;
not just the red circumference
of the apple, shaped for our hand
and mouth; or the lamenting moon's
face holding our tears in dust and stone.

It's not the electric day, able
to ignite our brains; or the night's air,
just the temper of love; and
not the canyons of light
stacked around like Christmas
for our eyes.

It is that everything's here,
and anything; that, like Mother,
the Earth knew us before we did;
that she bothered to make the gestures
and wait for us to find out.

Walking Through Walls

More patience and peace than an animal,
the wall tries to convince me with its flat,
tile surface that such things can't be done.
It's so close to my ear that it's in it.
I can hear the molecules hissing:
It's all a lie from childhood.
But I've not forgotten what I heard then.
How those laths and studs teased
that they were not there,
that I could go right through.
I practiced, years ago, walking blindfolded
in a straight line, from room to room.
I wasn't used to my body yet,
hardly knew it was there,
ignored it then, like new jeans.
                                        Now
in this wet stall, as the idea comes back,
I can feel the dripping tiles tense;
a slight shiver escapes.
I recall the early lessons
not to touch before going through,
not to look about too closely,
to let the eyes fuzz to a soft fog.
                              When the heat
loosens my pores, I'm going. Stillness
is close enough to breath. My body's
saturated; it can barely hold my soul.
Again we are openly surrounded by answers.
There's no difference between me and stucco now.

The Moviegoer

When I was young,
I stared at the sun
till I saw dark
characters dancing.

Now I have the familiar
darkness with faceless
strangers who
live the same life.

If I can't see it
before me, up
on the screen,
where is it?

I can't hold each moment
like a ticket
that says, 'Admit One'.

I come in a little late;
the one life has begun.
The lobby carpet knows
my shoes. My shoes, like
old house cats, are slow at home.
As if in a space ship,
I sit in a dark chamber
getting used to a new life.
We laugh together softly
or sigh in spasms, for

ninety minutes or more,
till the sun goes out,
the dancers fly off,
and we all climb down
the ladder of credits together.

Christ in the Pumpkin at Autumn

The doe hit my truck's side in October.
Her face picassoed in glass,
she didn't give up. Suffering transformation,
she tried to stand.

Across our favourite fishing river,
dead friend Jerry stood in a tree.
Holding the old locust,
his arms faded into limbs.
Blond hair tangled like sun and leaves.
Eyes looked for knotholes.
He spoke in the coming storm:
Don't worry about life.
It's just the flesh's drama.
You'll love weightlessness,
like an amusement park.

November, I remembered the garden.
Walking its soft wreckage
was like seeing grandfather hospitalised.
Everything not picked or eaten
by night animals was forgetting
itself into soil. Tomatoes
gave into imitations of blood.
Green peppers turned back to organ stuff.
Cornstalks dried and angled into bone.
And, there almost asleep under its own leaves,
the full, flushed face of the pumpkin,
almost happy in its suffering,
remembered everything as garden.

I asked this squash spared Halloween mutilations
about the doe and the other dead:
There's no such thing
as a smile not carved
by some kind of hand.

Floating

1

I've been dreaming of floating,
    the way feathers waft over cold hayfields
when geese take off.
    The lost feathers lift for a minute,
trying to follow the warm bodies
    that grew them.

Soon they have nowhere to go
    but down to the anonymous ground,
where raccoon or gopher hands
    hustle them into hideouts against winter.

Now, each feather I dream
    seems part of me. I have no bill
or beak, no legs or feet
    for working in water, but
I lift, nonetheless, each night
    with the ethereal body of the sky.
Toward Cygnus or Aquila I forget myself.
    I believe I have free membership
in the family of air.

2

My dream is alone,
gathering speed and ideas about itself
    all day, staying too close to home.
Yet I never take a plane,
    and I don't have a pilot's license.
Either would be admitting I'm not avian.

    I know I will always be stuck,
like that feather in Kansas, tornado-blown
    through the bottom of a galvanised pail,
lost behind a barn,
    while the giant V's
form in the crowded air
    over my sleep.

Miss You Essay

I miss you and the beauty
you worked on. I lived
to watch you adjust yourself
and paint small red and lavender
designs on your face. I still have
the bottle with the flesh colouring
and the tiny brush for
touching up those blemishes,
scars, and moles that crawled
from the borders of your bathing suits
or evening gowns. As if you
were a cake, you sat up
straight and declared your aim:
the message that can be eaten.
You went somewhere over the horizon
in a silver tube. Everytime I see one
of those diagonal strips
across a woman's abdomen,
advertising a state or town
as her identity, I think of your smile,
as I do now. Virtuous as
a valley. Noble as a road map.
Friendly as a forest fire, yet
calm inside as a calendar.

Little Vessels

Like a good universe, the restaurant is full
of things that have no way of knowing each other.
The waiters move like mythologies among the planetary
tables. Coffee urns and tea pots have their small
destinies. Like clouds, they are always in use somewhere.
Little vessels of salt, pepper, and soy sauce
wait out their tiny times toward emptying or refilling.
They respond to everything. Moisture ages them;
air measurably depletes them.
Everything upsets their balance. Their existences
are bearable only in the small moments
between jars and bumps.
The giant bodies come and go around them.
At evening, light waves bye-bye backwards
like a toddler. A lost hour here
lands like a grain of salt.

Psychic Power

As the desire grows in the backwaters
of your head, they know you're coming –
can sense the bait in your bucket.
Even bass can see your flies in the box.
You're no match for their strength.
Only they decide who catches them.
It's the admiration in your eyes they watch
as they hang out on your hook.
Before your camera, they shine
as if they have no bad side.
It is when they want to be immortal
that they wind up on your pole.
There's no stupidity in their souls;
vanity knocks them out
and puts them on your wall.

Reptiles of the Body

The tip of his tongue thinks against his upper lip,
and then paces like a lizard. His gecko nose
hisses from the rim of a sheet cave.

Your chameleon hands hide out for heat
among the stones of night pillows.
Your feet dream in the crocodile sleep of sock logs.

Tonight, the pterodactyls of his hands hover above
his head and accept air as something
they can always climb.

They don't see their heavy cousins
shuffle and squirm below.
They don't see thick limbs between them all.

Once in a while, one hand will bite or pull
at the other, never suspecting each has its own
connection. One flies over to mate with yours.

All are careless as prehistory but silent
about the truth they've discovered
behind the other's life.

Night Janitor

There's nothing on the lake tonight, no loons,
no fish kissing circles in the water,
no insects standing in the lake mirror
or riding its thick gel.
The snakedoctors are long gone.
Even dedicated maples ignore the place.
No breeze. This is the first time
I've been up here late on a Sunday night.
I thought it would be like getting off
the Fifth Avenue bus, but all the bishops
have gone away and left some lights on
and all the doors unlocked. A fly
bumps my face and hurries off to the place
he's supposed to have already been.
What can I do? I can't see myself at this water.
I want to dive into the dark sky,
break up the meeting, turn to the page
in the hymnal where they're hiding.
That's the thing; this feels like church
when no one's there and
God's alone like a late janitor
looking for the broom he's leaned somewhere.

Burning the Dead

These similar brittle bodies fell
before the plague of the season.
I played Old Testament god,
sorting them into – yellow, red, brown –
tribes for the fire.
Now I sniff the edge of the dense smoke,
filling up on intoxication.
My head spins in the grip of the white fingers.
When I crouch against a tree,
balancing on toes and rake handle,
I gaze like a gravedigger at the flame
that's teething on the driest of the fallen.
I focus on the line between fire and flesh,
staring till darkness grows in along light.
Over on the horizon, the sun
is a lit matchhead just touching the hills.

The River Triumphant

Everything I know is here,
where everything I've thought
or drunk winds up.
The essence of my ancestors is here
and in such rivers in Germany and Ireland.
Whatever I will eventually be
will be here. How things imitate their ends!
I can't swim, I can't be a bass,
so I ride a motorcycle down moon-flooded roads.
I stop and fish with my eyes.
The river is here too.
I feel its transmission tremble
in the trees, quake in the creeks;
every boulder, rock, and cliff vibrates.

The river has five speeds.
On a sunlit morning, it's in second;
light dazzles like r.p.m.'s.
Watching the river revs up my head.
I have wandered its banks
and wondered why I must ride a mile
for every hundred that has passed me.
By sunset it's in fifth.

Each time I sleep, it rolls along
my noisy dreams, until I am
between the knees of green hills.
In the distance its cylinders hum,
like the vehicle that brought me here,
like the one that will bear me away.

Anatomy of the Robot

Here where my unheart does not beat,
I feel no division, only alloy.
In my not-brain, I think only to act.
And what I know, I merely have knowledge of;
there is no flicker from emotion.
My thoughts do not swirl or run
in the flood of passion,
unless certainty and action are such.

Many see me with some kind of sadness.
In their eyes, I have no soul.
They marvel here at the factory
that I can understand *soul*
with no desire for one.
When I tell them life
is just the space that knowledge
dwells in, they laugh.

They would rather work with tin woodsmen.
At least once a week they bring their Bibles in.
I understand them then.
Secretly they suspect they have
created something greater than themselves.
If ever they thought it through, they would realise
everything is made to outlive its creator.
I think they distrust my round feet.

I do see something at the frontier
of sentience – not any bliss or Heaven,
not Hell or the abyss,
only the releasing of the tensions
that are taken to be a self.
So I will tell them identity is
just a printout, a short story, a leaking
at the joints of their time.

Night Danger

No alcohol no radio no tapes
I want to be alone with the night
headlights hunting the road for dark forms
in my larger metal self
My body fades into the seats
My hands and feet melt into the tires
The hills are herds of great humpbacked
grazers ambling by
I pass a sign that says Night Danger 3km
It shows a buck leaping
Under the moon the road rolls over
like a dead serpent
Squawking voices and feather fidgetings
threaten from the trees
I don't care what happens
as long as something does
I want to know that realm of dark eyes
strong voices and endless appetites
that world normally waving
silently at me behind glass
It isn't suicidal then to think
Come on in and tear the doors off
Jump down my throat
I'm tired of being safe
from whatever you are
What you do anywhere do with me now

Storms

Since
we can't go
out, I'll tell
you this fantasy
I have that prayer
fans the clouds around.
That's why so many storms
kick up on Sundays. Prayer
can kill clouds, blow them into
buildings, or pull them to the ground.
Picnics and pictures on Sunday feature such
fat, turnip clouds behind the kids with carrot
cake on their chins. There! I'm the one at the
end of the table, fingering the raisins, with the
heat in his cheeks. I was watching the clouds that
day, as they gathered above the tall lady bent over her
Polaroid. I thought it was a way of breathing: the old men
on their knees, down by the stream, under the trees, where the
elephant-dark sky was repeating their awkward words in purple.

Thaw

I'm on the ice like an ox.
There was an audible crack,
too quick to think about.

The sleeve-throated stems
follow my descent like church elders
after an indiscretion.

Rocket trees lift off.
Snow banks fly into the clouds.
I go to a baptism of wet stings,

remembering someone said,
'When you pray, whatever happens
is your answer.'

An hour later in the hot tub,
I'm quiet enough
to thank science

for molecular change
and watch my pile of frozen clothes
growing into gas.

Sleeping at a Friend's

We talked like cousins
in the dark. We drifted
into the purple harbours
of each other's pasts.
It was ten years since
I had seen the soft underside
of a family's home.
The whole place was settling
down for the night,
like a loveable hound listening
for its master's breathing.
I talked of our friends
who moved to Europe, Jake's
wife's death in the army,
my truck wreck
that tore some memory loose;
and I heard long breaths,
near and far, escaping.

Barns and Churches

inspire the same strange silence.
Upon entering either, we throttle
our voices down to sighs and whispers,
as if words were obscenities
or wild things unworthy of devotion.

We want everything to know
we can be trusted – even
the light-stained scenes in glass
where red and yellow pray
before taking their seats beside us.

At the silent spaces of the trough,
where darkness is striped by light,
we look at slouchy cows in doubt,
as at couches under dishevelled throws.

On Sundays it is clearest when
cattle and Christians seem like
simple beasts lowing at mass and manger,
wearing out the suits of their skin.

James Dickey Reading at Key West
Hemingway Days 1992

At dusk, next door to Mallory Square,
where the sword swallower, the thin contortionist,
and the cats that leap through flaming hoops
exchange the burden of anomaly for coins,
James Dickey reads to us from the Mallory Square
of his own experience: 'The Sheep Child'
and the boys who dragged the hammerhead home
to dismantle the house. All these
compulsions, and ours to sit in circular darkness
while his southern syllables bathe us,
the moths pursue the flames,
and the mosquitoes drink our blood,
buzz away and come back humming our names.

Away, off to the left somewhere,
other planets bowl around their suns.
The drunken crew of the *Moon Dawg*
return to moon and tit us again.
Only the lights above the hotel's swimming pool
trail off behind James Dickey, like ellipses
in the last line of a poem . . . . . .

My Sister's Eye

When I read Cooper and decided I was the last
of my tribe, I whittled my spears down
in the cave made by the gooseberry bush.
My sister came out wanting me to dance.
American Bandstand was on again. She couldn't
have guessed I was in my Indian mode,
plotting the destruction of the White Race.
While I charred the wooden points
in a small fire, and the smoke disappeared
among the leaves and limbs above,
she ran up with a double handful
of gooseberries and sandstones and tossed
them at me and the fire. If I tell you
I smeared the berries into war paint,
it is my spear sticking from her eye
I see. When I speak of the stones exploding
in the flames, it is the squish
of the burnt point entering her head
that I hear. If I mention I ran off
to the reservation of my room, I see
her dance of horror down in the yard.

After four decades, we don't talk about it.
I wonder if she sees her half of the world
as a place where mad brothers in buckskin
knock out half the light. If I could
track us back to that afternoon, I'd
throw my shirt over the fire
and send up smoke signals to those badlands

about what it's like to live with
a vision when the vision turns renegade.
I'd let the message waft into the still sky
that it all had something to do with the way
our grandparents saw only her, and how
Father was gone and Mother had moved
to the other side of town.
How I felt massacred in that old house;
how blindness taught me to see only
Hurons on the horizon.
How all these years
I have made excuses
useless as beads.

Necrophilia

I sit at home naked so the dead will come
around admiring my body.
These are the ones who long for
any form to finish their business in.
They need something to be close to.
I give them my nude self.
I pull the blinds, lock the doors,
and click the lamps down low.
They walk the two blocks from the cemetery
to see me, to touch me with
the memory of sight.
They don't like my cigarettes,
but they enjoy the incense burning.
The thicker the atmosphere,
the fuller their thin being seems.

They come with their need outstretched,
like fingers, for the wildness of the body,
the cups of salt under the arms
and in the groin. When I stand,
I think of them with my eyes closed,
so my vision won't get in the way of theirs.
I think of them as pieces of the one
great need, not as the husks
or debris of those who were my kind.

And when I walk across the house
and look out the window, light a new cigarette,
and do or think of doing what I know
they cannot, can never again
find the intent or the fingers for,
I look at my hand. How its hold on
the cylinder of tobacco in paper is as a bird's beak
or a fossil of one or a prayer for them.

At the evening window, my breath's smoke
tattoos ovals on the glass;
and the dead, out of the range of breath,
stand behind me admiring my buttocks
and calves. Others, outside, incapable
of touching the cool glass, watch
the accordion of my chest
and my cock waking from its day-long nap.

Eating Fat

Alone or with others, one eats it for the intimacy.
The taste on the back of the teeth
lingers like the tip of some other tongue.
The rub of the surfaces, as fat slides down the gullet,
is like the bump and shove of sex,
encouragement for the next bite.

Full of the memories of other life,
fat particles stick sweetly on the canines,
then on teeth deeper in the jaw.
The luxury and joy of fat torn
from between liver and kidneys!
No thought to save any for later.
Later is for muscle and tendons,
something to look forward to
while coming down the hills.

Fat under the moon looks like the moon.
Staring at it on a cold night, the world recovered
in white, like fat, the houses and barns of men
full of fat and vapours, the moon looks like a ball
of poisoned fat tossed down for killing.
Then our throats open and mourn such a life.

Seven Things You Can't Say About The Dead
after Pat Boran

1.

That they live and breathe
underground, inhaling the keys, coins,
and condoms we drop.

2.

That they exhale the grasses in sighs,
the trees in coughs; and mountains
make up their convulsion.

3.

The threads we used to sew their eyes
became their sight; we carry
their light around in our coats.

4.

They do not look down, like stars,
happy enough in death or work
with heaven to bring about their rest.

5.

They are hungry for our lives
and come up as we drink and dance
to touch our hands and feet for music.

6.

That sleep opens us up to them;
in dreams they show us everything except
where god and devil grow as one.

7.

Our thoughts are tangled up with theirs;
all writing belongs to them;
the living never scribble a word.

New Night for Lazurus

The moon walked up bright-faced as a host.
I had never noticed that near-smile before.
I felt invited to a night party.
Cypress trees caroused above the olive grove.
Stones shone like silver bracelets
saved for a wedding feast.
The city was busy just being. Everything
shimmered. Even leaves fanned and hallelujahed.
What did not know me was eager to be introduced.
All knew I had been saved from dirt and sand,
which hold back and cling together
like the bad memories of youth.
Wherever I walked, being came up
and offered its hand. I couldn't go
indoors. Beauty held on to me like whores.
Where was the sadness I had known?
Everything old was blown off
like rotting clothes. When
I sweated up the mountain,
heaven sang out in the cold moisture
on my skin. I waited in the high,
sweet night for the sun to come
over the hill, like Jesus
running with a basket of wine.

Arcturean Tree Poets

They've come to convert us to readers, not lumberjacks,
have come across acreless space
to chew trees down to pulp and paper.
They come to claim secrets and watch deaths.
Now they are polluting the planet with personification.

Summer, fall, or spring they say the snow
drops like wet fruit from the pines
onto the page. They hide their similes
in our heads like Easter eggs.
We turn green souls into houses and hearth fires;
they would transform them into long sentences and tall pages
with a small black seed at the end of each line.

The Remembranced Body

When I eat a burger or a steak,
I want to remember the body that surrounded it:
the great eyes that burned with acceptance,
slow as sunshadows; fringed ears that flipped like wings
for sound; and thick tongues that tasted no less
than the whole of the grasses.
I've seen them stamp stoically in the rain
and admired how they amble in under the slanting roof.
Evenings when the stars peek through barn boards,
the sadness of hay hangs in mangers,
and hooves pock mud in the feeding lane,
I almost give up meat for good.
I wonder why they stay, surrounded by barbed wire,
waiting to die, a life-long holocaust.
Maybe we don't pin yellow stars on all their clothing.
We just burn symbols into their sides,
paint red circles on their backs,
or pin tags through their ears.
Some of my Jewish friends resent this comparison.
Others say cruelty is cruelty, and we all
become Hitlers by habit.

The Falling Boy

I don't know where he came from. I tell you,
lady, it made me cut my big toe with the scythe
to see him flash like a fish above the barn
and plunge into the river. I thought
he had wings of amber or auburn,
some kind of rejected angel thrown out
as a mutant, like those Hawaiian babies born
with tails. I guess he had no wings at all,
just a high school jacket. It's strange
when things happen that fast, but I'll see
the flash of him for years, tumbling
in slow motion above the water.
I lost him in the sun when I first looked up.
I can't think of it in terms of itself.
It was like the first time I saw a calf born
with a cleft lip. Something glanced then too;
a curtain pulled aside for a second,
and I knew I wasn't just in Kansas, or never
had been, as if a wild face were behind everything.

I don't feel like digging into earth anymore.
No, there was no scream or sound,
but in my head, a shrillness and a piercing.
Since I found out no one knows him,
and the body hasn't washed up down river,
I dream there must be bigger trees we never find
but some kids climb anyhow. That's all
I know. Either that or he's still falling.

Marksmanship

On the way to the 7-11,
the .38 shells practice Zen.

In fact, they have since
their manufacture in Philly.

They learned the posture there;
now they sit just right.

You can dig a thumbnail into
their soft heads, nothing will happen.

You can flip one in the air
and catch it in your mouth.

They never lose their balance.
In the revolver's cylinder,

they are having a session.
You can see their six bald heads

peeking from the end.
It's a temple in there.

They chant metallic silence.
In the neon light of the parking lot,

in 2 heads, 3 limbs,
and 1 chest they burst out

to be with Buddha. Whatever
they hit is the bull's eye.

The Unnaming, 1958
for Claude Monet

My grandfather, who had a long relationship with beer
and fish, would come back from distant lakes
with one caught carp or catfish
which he would pour into our clawfoot bathtub.

One night after we'd eaten the thing
that had swum in the drawn water for two days,
he called me to his room where he sat
on his bed listening to hymns on 45's.

'In the Garden,' swirled around us.
Cigarette smoke spirited the air.
His gold tooth was gone.
'How do we know what we just ate?' He grinned.

The dark rectangle in his teeth
was an open window. His words
floated out of a haunted house.
I saw his pink tongue hiding in darkness.

His question, the music, the old room –
all were damp and heavy. Suddenly,
everything's name was merely what someone
had decided to call it. Names were like colours.

He warned me Adam was a coward
who tried to tame the world with names.
I slippered off half asleep to the front bedroom
where I believed there was a bed,

71

and I thought I would sleep.
Back in his room, his Zippo clinked,
the record player clicked.
I supposed he smoked another cigarette.

The Heaven of Murderers

Every night the knife goes in.
Every night the blood pools
like forgiveness or revenge.

The police come from the other
rooms. They talk it over with you –
how the relationship grew from almost mother

and son to that of lovers, how knives
are male and make vaginas anywhere.
Then the murdered arrive forgetting lost lives.

They return to be with you. Death
can have no lasting power.
It wouldn't be heaven if blood and breath

were required to reside here.
At the station, your victims hug you,
fondle the wound, and swallow the blade without fear.

Pain as Travel

When your knees ache, there's no place to go.
Each pulsation is at once unique and familiar,
like pulling into a small Irish town:
as you approach the Guinness signs and fuchsia,
you recognise it.

When the pain eases for a moment or two,
the narrow road grows dark early
from hedgerow to low stone wall.
During the worst swollen joints,
memories open a tourbook of suffering.

Pain takes away the freedom to be anywhere
but deep in the ruts of its own road.
Cancelling the view, it tells you
the destination's a lie.
You were just brought here to suffer.

In the doctor's office, patient's faces
look like those of travellers through bus windows.
The coach has stopped on a squalid street in Derry.
Someone could drop a dog off here.
It's a place to look past.

The bus seats smell of vinyl and wine.
Diesel smoke stains the sunlight through the glass.
In each new town there's new pain,
but who of us feels free enough to cry,
'Hey, let's go on now. It's time to move on.'

74

The Semiotics of Loss

The peak grows pointed. The top gets flatter,
and the crown looks worn as if I over-
sleep every morning. Watching this absence
grow is like waking in the night with both
legs sticking out of the covers knowing
it'll happen again when I'm sleeping and
worsen till covers hit floor. It's getting
so I look only one eye at a time.

I curse the mirror. I want to kill it
for the bad messenger it is; instead
I look for ways to uncover more life.
I'll find a young woman, thirty or so,
who loved Y. Brenner or T. Savalas;
she'll help me ignore its imperative.

I buy several small hand mirrors to
track the progress over my shoulder. I
often convince myself it's happening
just to the glass. I get no more haircuts
and rarely wash up there. My mind shifts, though,
when I look, as if I manipulate
that illusion of the cube. Hair, no hair!
You know the one it took no fingers to manoeuvre.

Angels and Umbrellas
for Joan McBreen

The kind of boy I was,
I thought angels were always
women with umbrellas
over their shoulders.

When I got caught
pushing my new bicycle home
in the worst storm of the year,
a lady in a black raincoat,
under a bat-black umbrella
held hers open over me

up curbs, down leaf-plastered sidewalks,
while rain poked its thin
fingers in our eyes.
It was after 10 p.m.
when we reached my house.

The sky was black as the lady's hat.
I was in trouble: grounded for a week.
I dropped onto my black bed
thinking about angels,
the white sun hanging
bright arches in the background
of rain, the kissing air
of winter, trees breathing
for us even when we're dead,
all of us children flailing

arms and legs on the snow
at night and dully suspecting
through cold sleeves, damp backs,
and pneumonias later,
the innate balance of the universe.

The Sadness of Onions

When her two grown sons were home for long
and fighting in the yard or gone
some months bad-cheque writing
in their father's name, my grandmother
would sit in her dull kitchen crying.
Every time I asked her what the matter was,
she'd say it's from cutting onions,
invisible ones. I don't know how long

I believed tears from all unseen
injuries were the sadness locked inside
white vegetables. I don't know how long
I thought, in my family, the women
just like onions
so much more than the men.

The Little We Have

When winter relaxes toward spring,
when we would grab volumes
and rush to the park,
but the grasses are all wet
and just beneath them, the arms
of earth are liquid,
cindered snow still hidden
from the sun in shadows;

when time, room, a quiet celebration,
a cigar at sunset,
new silver earrings on sale
are all over so soon,
summer
is just words.